Ocean Biome

Written by
Shirley Duke

Rourke
Educational Media

ourkeeducationalmedia.com

Scan for Related Titles
and Teacher Resources

www.rourkeeducationalmedia.com

PHOTO CREDITS: Cover: stephan kerkhofs; Title Page © Zhukov; Page 4 © Eric Isselee and Merkushev Vasiliy; Page 5 © James W. Photography and VanHart; Page 6 © Specta; Page 6a © worldswildlifewonders; Page 7 © Kasparart; Page 9 © Marzanna Syncerz; Page 10 NOAA; Page 11 © Clinton Hastings; Page 12 © melissaf84; Page 13 © Shannon Heryet; Page 14 © Bruno Ismael Stacy Barnett; Page 15 © Øystein Paulsen; Page 16 © trekandshoot; Page 17 © Danette Anderson; Page 18 © angelo lano; Page 18a © worldswildlifewonders; Page 19 © Vladimir Melnik; Page 19a © Kim Briers, Brendan Hunter; Page 20 © Rich Carey; Page 21 © Hurst Photo

Edited by Jill Sherman

Cover design by Renee Brady
Interior design by Nicola Stratford bdpublishing.com

Library of Congress PCN Data

Seasons of the Ocean Biome / Shirley Duke
(Biomes)
ISBN 978-1-62169-895-1 (hard cover)
ISBN 978-1-62169-790-9 (soft cover)
ISBN 978-1-62717-002-4 (e-Book)
Library of Congress Control Number: 2013936811

Also Available as:

Rourke Educational Media
Printed in the United States of America,
North Mankato, Minnesota

Rourke
Educational Media

rourkeeducationalmedia.com
customerservice@rourkeeducationalmedia.com • PO Box 643328 Vero Beach, Florida 32964

Table of Contents

Deep and Shallow

What is the ocean like? Saltwater waves pound the shore. The ocean might look empty from your view on dry land. But it is filled with life.

Oceans have:

✓ Salt water.
✓ Shallow and deep water zones.
✓ Warm and cold temperatures.
✓ Many kinds of plants and animals.

Seal

Arctic Ocean

Atlantic
Ocean

Pacific
Ocean

Indian
Ocean

Southern Ocean

The World's Oceans

You may see **algae**, or seaweed, drifting on top of the water. Some life swims in the water. Other kinds ride the ocean waves.

Shallow coral reefs, aquatic plants, and **kelp** forests use the Sun to make food.

Kelp

Did you know that sunlight cannot reach the deep ocean floor? The deep water stays cold. Yet, deep water has life suited for the dark ocean bottom.

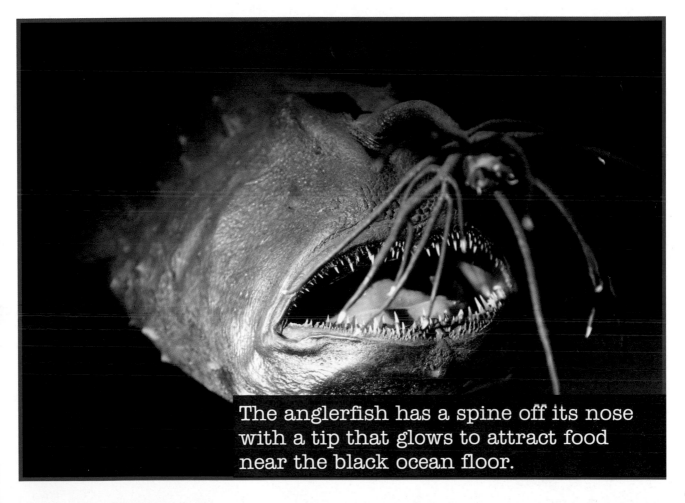

The anglerfish has a spine off its nose with a tip that glows to attract food near the black ocean floor.

Earth Tilts!

Earth **tilts** as it spins to make day and night. Summer comes when Earth tilts toward the Sun. It warms the top of the water.

In the summer, the Sun shines longer, which lets plants make more food. **Phytoplankton** live in the oceans. These tiny plants feed much of the life in oceans. They make food using the Sun's light.

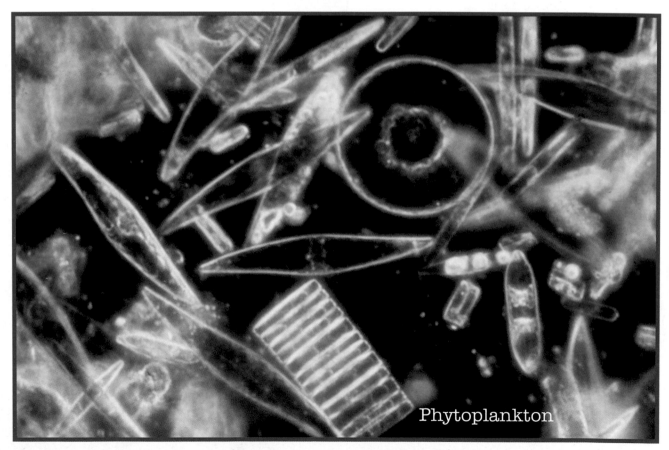

Phytoplankton

Animals move to the cooler water near the poles in summer. Why? More food lives there.

Humpback Whale

Whales move to cold water in summer. They follow their food north.

Fall Changes

Days grow shorter in fall. The water begins to cool. Some animals return from the cold waters in the north. Whales move to warmer water to have their babies in the fall.

To have their babies, whales must leave the cool feeding waters before they turn icy cold.

In the fall, **salmon** leave the ocean. They swim up river to lay eggs.

Watch Out for Winter!

Winter storms come. High winds make waves. Ice forms in the north. Crabs move to deep water. Their claws grip the muddy bottom.

Ocean Crab

Some mammals and fish follow food like algae, **krill**, and small fish south in winter. Then they have their young there.

Krill

Animals of all sizes, including small fish, penguins, seals, and whales, feed on krill.

New Life

In spring, longer days make sea grass grow tall. Algae blooms grow in the warm days.

Sea Grass

In springtime, fish like flounder return to shallow water near shore. Shellfish lay their eggs there. Birds wade to look for tiny fish.

Looking like the ocean floor helps flounders hide from predators.

Some marine animals stay in the same place all year.

Sea otter

Sea otters stay near the same kelp beds. They leave only to hunt. Harbor seals do not leave their homes.

Harbor seals

Animals have **adapted** to live in their ocean homes.

Walruses have blubber to stay warm. Giant clams with colored algae open wide for sunlight in coral reefs.

The Future of Oceans

Oceans seem so big that nothing could harm them. But the ocean holds life that can be harmed with small changes. People sometimes do things that cause problems.

What can you do to help our oceans? The small changes you make can help save our oceans.

You Can Help
Protect Oceans:
✓ Reduce carbon in the air by riding in cars less.
✓ Recycle plastic.
✓ Eat farm-raised fish.
✓ Help clean up beaches.

Recycling plastics keeps it from ending up in our oceans.

Study Like a Scientist
Find the Salt

1. Put salt water in a flat dish.

2. Put it in a sunny place.

3. Watch the water for a few weeks.

4. Do you see the salt?

5. Add more water and try again.

The water evaporates like that in the ocean. It leaves salt. Adding water acts like rain on the ocean.

Glossary

adapted (uh-DAPT-uhd): made a change to fit a different condition

algae (AL-gee): a life-form that can make food like a plant but has no roots or stem

kelp (KELP): a large brown algae, also known as seaweed

krill (KRIL): a tiny animal that looks like a shrimp

phytoplankton (FYE-toh-plahnk-tuhn): tiny plants that make the most food for ocean life

salmon (SAM-uhn): a fish with silver skin and pink insides

tilts (TILTS): leans or tips so something is not straight up and down

Index

Websites

kids.nceas.ucsb.edu/biomes/index.html

www.montereybayaquarium.org

sealevel.jpl.nasa.gov/education/stuffforkids

About the Author

Shirley Duke has written many books about science. She lives in Texas and New Mexico and loves the different seasons in each place. She likes exploring along the beaches in Texas and finding oyster beds. Some of her favorite foods come from the ocean, and also fish farms.

Meet The Author!
www.meetREMauthors.com